HIGH
ON
RUST

Ray Webber
Selected Poems

'A hangover is better than a madhouse'
Charles Bukowski

I dedicate my poems to my nephew Ken Hallett whose considerable talents have been thwarted by chronic illness. And I extend my deepest thanks to Steve Bush for his enthusiasm and sheer hard work. My thanks also to Richard Jones for his work and encouragement, and to Fiona Williams and Corin Bush for their kind support.

High on Rust
First published 2016 by Tangent Books

Tangent Books
Unit 5.16 Paintworks
Bristol BS4 3EH
0117 972 0645
www.tangentbooks.co.uk
Email: richard@tangentbooks.co.uk

ISBN 978-1-910089-41-5

By Ray Webber

Poems selected by Steve Bush

Design: Joe Burt; cover art: Ray Webber;
Ray Webber photograph: Roger Hicks

Thanks to: Johanna Darque, Roger Ball, Corin Bush, Asif Khan,
Andrew Giles

I've been invited to say something about my poems. No can do. They must stand up for themselves. This does not diminish my gratitude for the generous praise made by others.

Ray Webber, 2016

Ray Webber
Biographical Notes

Ray Webber was born in 1923 in Redcliffe, Bristol, to Welsh parents, Charles Webber and Kate Regan. His father was a left-wing activist and his mother a Catholic. The family lived in poverty and Ray had a poor education leaving school at the age of 14. When he was 18 he was conscripted into the army to fight in the Second World War. He left the army in 1946 and it was during his final year in uniform that he began writing poetry.

His earliest work was influenced by Shelley, Keats, Byron, Tennyson and the Romantics, culminating in a Dylan Thomas phase extending into the Fifties. He continued studying literature and art in his spare time and became intrigued by the work of T.S. Eliot. At first he struggled to understand Eliot's verse, but as he continued his studies, he came to appreciate Eliot's avoidance of poetic conceits and the originality of the writing became more clear. Eliot, who Webber regards as the first great modernist, remains his single biggest influence.

"As I began to understand Eliot, he became a major figure in my life," says Ray. "I became determined that everything I wrote would be different from everything I read." Ezra Pound's literary criticism strengthened

Ray's resolve. In the 50s and 60s, Ray discovered the Beat Generation – poets Ginsberg, Kerouac, Gregory Corso, and the novelists William Burroughs and Ken Kesey – which fuelled his life-long admiration of modern American literature.

In 1974 Ray was able to take early retirement from his job as a postman and concentrate fully on his research and writing. Ray is entirely self taught. All of the work in this book is from that period onwards.

Ray also cites Sartre, Kafka, Dostoyevsky and in particular the New York poets Frank O'Hara, John Ashbery and others as significant influences on his literary taste. His world outlook is atheistic: "The Catholic church and schools cured me of my religion," says Webber. Sartre's fiction and philosophical works form the basis of his view that our existence is accidental, not necessary.

I've been close to Ray Webber's work for so many years that I can't be wholly objective about it. Fortunately, poetry comes in many styles and degrees of intensity. There are no absolute criteria. So I can confidently express my opinion that Ray Webber is one of this country's most profound, thought-provoking and entertaining poets.

You won't have to delve too far into this collection to realise why I've been of this opinion for more than 40 years, and I'm not the only one to feel this way. Ray is now 93. It's taken nearly a lifetime of 'backing into the limelight' for this collection of his poetry to come to fruition, but it's been more than worth it. This selection is but a fraction of the work he's created. It is intended to give an impression of the many facets of his writing, its original thought and subversive edge.

Steve Bush, 2016

Contents

Invitation

come on in and sit down
have a cigarette
a drink
what would you like to talk about?
being stabbed through the heart
stabbed in the back
being swindled
rejected
humiliated
bored with routine
confused and exasperated by bureaucracy
dissatisfied disillusioned
disgusted with yourself
i'll listen if it helps
but beyond that
i can't do anything for you
i can't change the world
i can't change human nature
if i had that sort of power
i'd go raving mad
anyone can go
slighty round the bend
you've only got to look at me
but the madness that comes from power
does not sit in a squalid room

revising last week's poems
and tearing up poems
from the week before that –
'the lunatic the lover and the poet'
okay it has a good ring
but even the great bard
got things wrong sometimes
none of us are perfect
and those who counsel perfection
are mad lunatics of the first order
the lunatics you've got to watch out for
they often sit behind big desks
tortured by the conviction
that they're surrounded
by treacherous scoundrels
disguised as woolly-headed poets
dreamy lovers
and disaffected nonentities
you know all the rest
how heads roll and
spirits are broken

next time
if you come around again
we may talk about Gurus
fundamentalist preachers
and the new politics of correctness
flourishing in so-called democracies

The beautiful miracle of childbirth

my real name
is Mervin Derryberry Grubcock.
my father was a part-time docker
and a full-time anarchist.
my mother was a full-time domestic slave
and a double-time catholic saint.

i was born 1923 Bristol central slums
in a street that went by the nickname
Dry-rot Terraces and Firetraps.

on the evening that my mother
went into what's known as labour
nothing was quite shipshape and Bristol fashion.
the bedbugs were crawling over everything
the backstreet midwife
arrived stinking drunk
and busted her nose on a tall iron bedpost.
my father slipped on the stairs
while carrying the boiling water
scalded his chest and fractured his wrist
and was carted off to hospital.

a prostitute was knifed
in a pub across the street.

a bomb went off in the blacksmiths' yard
and a man next door was arrested
on a charge of attempted necrophilia.

and while all this was going on
my mother was howling like a dog
and saying her rosary at the same time.

after the midwife had dragged me into the world
she drank another quarter of gin
and passed out puking in the shithouse.
neighbours cleaned the place up
and my father came home from casualty
with his arm in a sling
and a 2-pint flagon of stout
in each of his overcoat pockets.

after draining a flagon straight down
he said to me: Mervin old son
if we can survive a night like this
we can take all the shot and shell
this fucking battlefield of existence
or what they call life may throw at us.

of course we were all very young
and foolish at the time.
Rudolph Valentino ruled the world
and everyone was doing the tango.

as to whether my survival was a good thing
i've often had reason to doubt.

Orphan

when i got born
my father was hopping mad
he hopped skipped and jumped
in the back yard
crying joy oh joy
praise be to god for one more mouth to feed
and he drowned the tomcat in the rain butt.
my mother rubbed me down with goose fat
and swaddled me in old cheese cloths.
then she crooned me a little song
that went something like this:
if you don't be a good boy
the bogeyman will come and get you.
all my aunts and uncles
brought gifts of sheep's offal and decapitated chickens
they anointed my head with chicken's blood
and hung the stinking offal on the front door
to cast evil spells on the rent man.
then everybody dashed off to the cinema
to have a good laugh
at Charlie Chaplin's film called Easy Street.
i don't know
where they all went after that
and i ain't ever seen them since anyway
i'm still here

with seventy-one years gone by
talking and chuckling to myself
about what a bad boy i always was
and waiting for the bogeyman to come.

Easter poem

Many years ago I had a sister
who rose from the dead.
Oh, she said, I somehow knew
something like this would happen
and I'd all but wiped you all
from my memory.

That's what she said – suffused
with a mocking glow.
round the edge of her glaze.

Did you know you can fracture
your pelvis   or
feel a spear deep under your ribs
while cueing up a straight pocket
down at the Pig and Whistle

                    where
the old city used to stand as if
it were forever –
        and suddenly
the stars have never looked less
sanctimonious –
        and the tarantulas
of the mind become as inconsequential

as the jolly raconteurs
propping up bars all over the globe.

In remembrance

Of two special females in my life:
First an aunt
Much too young to be an aunt
Kind, pretty, vivacious
Used to sit me on her lap
Midst the scent of roses and violets
Sweetness, softness, gentleness.
She suddenly disappeared
Died in mysterious circumstances
There were whispers of drinking
Smoking and late nights
Madness, putrescence, other horrors
Unspeakable diseases contracted
Through her fatal fondness for men.

The second:
My younger sister and playmate
Died. Was buried. And her soul
Went to heaven at the age of five.
My mother wept. I wept.
My mother said: God's will.
My father said: Some fucking doctor
Buggered up a simple throat-swab.
My mother wept. I wept.
My mother spent hours looking out the window.

My father took to reading strange books
Late at night – awesome volumes.
He became a grim fanatical preacher
Of an optimistic futuristic doctrine
Called Marxist/Leninist Communism.

And none of us
Lived happily thereafter.

Truer than true

When I was a kid in my cot
Sucking my dummy
There was always lots of guys around
Calling each other comrade
And talking about capitalism, revolution
And the proletarian tatership.

When I was able to walk
My mother would often haul me off
To the cinema, in terrible rainstorms.
We watched tall handsome cowboys
Shooting down ugly red-indian fuckers.

My father would fly into a rage
And say movies are crap. Then he'd
Slap my mother cross the face –
And she'd call him a dirty bleedin' pig.

One evening, the comrades assembled.
The minutes of the previous meeting
Were read out and endorsed,
And they went through the agenda
Thoroughly and eloquently. Then the
Chairman called any other business.

Comrade chairman, I said, I wish
To move a resolution, as follows:
It takes more than a talking shop
To wipe out the dirty capitalist scum.
What we need is guns and horses
And somehow we have to become tall
Handsome angel-faced bastards.

Handsome bastards, said my mother,
That disqualifies your father for a start.
And, after a perfunctory discussion,
The motion was unanimously defeated.

The comrades drifted out quietly –
Though I'm sure i heard some one say
That little runt is a rabid fascist.

A little time a little vandalism

I've had it with the afterlife baloney
eternal bliss of the soul
in what's called the hereafter

and none of your fancy scientific jargon
about spacetime

if we're going to talk about time
we'll do it in strictly human terms

time is nothing more than a lifespan
and a lifespan is but a short distance
between being hatched and being trashed

i first had this intuition of time
when a mere twelve-year-old kid
undernourished and inadequately clad

i was in a sort of trance-like state
of sullen alienation sometimes called grace
attained through what may be described
as enforced self-abnegation and asceticism

and that was a good enough reason
for taking the hammer from the coal shed

and smashing up my debt-ridden father's
ugly old worm-eaten grandfather clock

Love story

Light years ago
In a city of canals, breweries
And a cigarette factory
I met a girl
Who excited me so much
I became a stranger to my friends.

Iron hoofs and iron-rimmed wheels
Clattered over granite cobbles.
I kissed her lightly on the mouth.
Her eyes popped out and she
Swallowed her bubble-gum.

Then I wrapped her in my arms
Discovered she had no bones
And her hair smelled of water
From the swimming baths.

Dusk was approaching.
The lamplighters with long poles
Hit the backstreets on their bicycles.
I groped for her little gizmo.

No, please, no, no, she cried.
So I flipped her upside-down.

Her knickers were immaculate blue-white
Her belly hot to the touch.
A sudden paralysis
Took hold of my asinine fingers.

My heart melted in its cage.
A news-vendor sang about Spain
The evening special, the echo
The ho ho of war.

A futile consultation

doctor, will you please help me.
i'm a menace to myself and the world.
If you promise not to interrupt, i'll explain.

The animal kingdom, mankind included,
is ruled by the insolent principal of male virility.
the world is plagued by rapacious male genitalia.
cock and balls dominate everything.
history is a cock and balls story.
the technology of war is a cock and balls story.
and as for optimistic futurism –
that's nothing but a cock-and bull story.

so having wised up to the male supremacist conspiracy
i took to casting my seed
rebelliously and randomly on the ground –
mostly alone, but sometimes with female collaboration.

then i realised this practice could cause
serious ecological damage.

so i switched to wanking into a handkerchief
and tossing it straight in the washing machine
with a generous helping of super-concentrated detergent
–

believing it would be
a more environment-friendly process.

but after further research it dawned on me
that human sperm laced with super detergent
is a very potent cocktail by any standards
and though it gurgles down the drain out of sight
it seeps back into the ecological system.

what a diabolocal merry-go-round, i thought,
the way i'm going on, i can't win.
This problem demands the most drastic action possible.

so now, doctor, i'll come to the point:
could you please arrange for me to undergo
a voluntary and irreversible castration.

i know it will be very expensive
and i'm aware of the economic situation –
so i'll pay for the operation myself
even if it means selling my teevee and stereo
and my grandfather's solid gold watch and chain
and giving up smoking tobacco and dope.

now please stop churning out your usual crap
about seeing a highly recommended psychiatrist –
it only re-affirms your authoritarian prejudices.

I've got used to being insane
and in fact i'm getting to enjoy it.
It's my testicles need shrinking – not my my head.
Thank you for wasting my time.

Love

God loves everybody. God loves
anything. God loves nasty slobs
always in a snit, singalong jocks
old crock grunts and groans
women with talking clits, women
who do pretty embroidery and
try to be nice to Red China.

My mother loved me too much though
she never said but only fixed me a
sidelong gaze of terrible female
wisdom. For my father to love you
you had to toe the Leninist line
and I never knew if I did.

I can't remember what my Aunty
Olive said when she wasn't chewing
red-hot coals but I knew she loved
a guy who shouted he was framed
every time he landed in the nick.

My uncle Wally had love shining out
of his arse. He always said to me
straighten up son shoulders back
walk like a man because I love you

you little shit. I guess he always
knew I was jerking off in the bath-
room and stealing his cigarettes.

Inconceivable

a truly great year
was the year 1970

i spread the arson news
and proudly wore my badges
FUCK CENSORSHIP
and
LONG LIVE GARBAGE PSYCHEDELICS

my father was dying
and i told him
do your own thing

while i did mine
down at the libertarian squat
with my cronies the cannabis cakes
swapping sex partners
and performing
electric meter bypass

my rip-off poem
EYEBALL COLLISIONS
was highly acclaimed
at the literary incest circle

life was
inconceivable
then
and it is still
only more so

my vision has improved with age

and whichever way i look
i see the ineffable
with fatuous clarity

A far cry

silence gushes out of
my mouth. if you want
fun and happy talk. go
watch the Kiddie Hour.
silence gushes out of my
mouth. and insofar as
we all struggle on. on-
ward to meet the one
certainty. you know ex-
actly what i mean. the
one and only certainty.
and no flashy talk can
alter that. but that's
not entirely what i mean
by silence gushes out of
my mouth.

silence gushes out of
my mouth. like we look
at the wind and try to
figure out how often it
kicks shin and stubs its
toes while dancing merr-
ily with the trees. yes
the wind that seeks no

approval. never strives
for merit marks. the wind
that cocks a snook at all
pedagogic set-ups. all
standards of excellence.
all knowledge right down
to elementary arithmetic.

to recap now on silence
gushes out of my mouth.
it's all wishful thinking.
perhaps an unattainable
dream. so i'll go for plain
gibberish. and that's no
small order by any criteria
of delinquency. congenital
idiocy aside. my sole and
ultimate ambition is to
talk and write utter gibberish. and i've only got
one life. of which there's
maybe one decade left. in
which to unlearn everything
and become as wild and
shameless as the merrily
waltzing wind.

Ambition

I wanted to be a sculptor in July
But I found myself painting Bristol South
For several weeks in August.
Is there a will to decipher in all seriousness
The riddle of the used car lots ?
For centuries I've clawed my way
Through mountains of wax or
They could have been vomited bananas
And dreamers mumbling and drooling.
I was sure I had it in me
To be a great musician, a composer
But I blew it through strumming on old bedsprings.
Now a blonde, waffle-mash sunrise sports
A nightmare's growth of foul breath
Nervous knives and solitude on furious casters
Hasten to a marshmallow ruin
And I throw a foamy flame.

Our necks are on the block and we're nibbling the straw in the basket

My father died
of Marxist revisionism.
I once asked him
what communism was.
Communism son he said
is sofa power plus
electric drills in the brain.
And democracy ? I said.
The beauty of democracy
he said
is dogshit in free fall
over hideous graveyard
sculpture and
no flowers by request.

After my father died
my mother vanished in
tales of the supernatural.
I once asked her
what a foetus was.
A foetus she said
is a dear little vampire
that lives in a woman's
belly –

and you
my little nosey parker
is an awful scruffy
barbarian.

Green toad jelly
props up the firmament.
My father never said that.
My mother never said it.
Maybe I said it
but I couldn't have
because
what I said was
I'm scared of young women
with pushchairs and dungarees
I'm lagging
behind my beginnings
and the smirking canker
is chewing up

all my pencils.

Poem to a plasticine carcass

Oh to have thought worth thinking
This concoction I'm knocking back
To render myself amenable to social life
Tastes like something brewed in a school lab
I'm a bona fide Anglo Saxon
Fully baptised Christian
Brought up to feel superior to foreigners
And pagans
A few more swigs of this tiger-piss
And maybe I'll chant mock Gregorian
The sun shines a buttercup
Under mother earth's chin
And she turns into a merry widow
Waiting for her meals on wheels
The ranters and shit street theatre artists
Who once scandalised suburbia
And drove many barbers to suicide
Are now a row of beans in the Tate or some such
There is no more near and far
Sedentary fingers on the zapper
We traverse the whole universe in an instant
Every day adds to what's gone
Subtracts from what's to come
Julie calls me illogical
Turds such as you

she says
And then she turns away
And talks to her potted plants
Maybe she has a point
Our absurd and fine endeavours
To make light of things already weightless
Contradictions dear to the heart
I once played a minor role
In a Marxist-Leninist
Revolution
That never happened

Goodbye to sigmund freud

In the beginning
was Oedipus because
the audience wanted blood.
The days before ballpens
easy options, fast food, microchips
soundbites.
While the trains were
running on time
to the gas chambers
I was swooning over Shelley and Keats
and longing to go insane
with a beautiful smile
and share a cup of suicide with Juliet.
It coulda been a great party
but everything went wrong.
Head to toe
I've lost an inch, my genitals
are in a coma
and due to some tragic flaw
in my nature
I can't figure out the symbolism
of losing my socks in launderettes.
True, I was a shit as a kid
slept with my mother
when my father was in jail

and I've never slept so well since.
 Tranquility
or as near as I can get
is a dandy yellow pill
TAKE ONE WHEN NEEDED. 2 or 3 for kicks.
 Freud died in 1939.
 Nobody's rocking my dreamboat.
 Goodnight Vienna, zombie hatstands
parental mucus.
 Freud died in 1939
just before the terrible catastrophe
that was born of splendour and discipline.

The bare-bones autobiography

at a fair guess I must have done
the average wearisome stint of ordinary living

that's to say, when not prostrate with introspection
or wrestling with a difficult text
or hijacked by nightdreams and daydreams
of somewhat heroic perversity

true, I tweaked a real nipple here and there
penetrated a vagina
achieved the odd orthodox orgasm

though my mother was the only woman
I ever managed to address in proprietorial terms

the Western World's belly
which was quite unremarkable in those days
is swollen now to a gross and critical mass

but who am I
to assume diagnostical airs?

estranged as I am
from everything, not least myself

bedevilled by irrational guilt

my innards docile and sluggish
except for the weekly laxative-induced cataclysm

who has never been first past the post
in anything other than petty and parochial

so come weird and otherworldly music
suck my head till it's brainless, weightless

for I have seen the elect
their faces... by the gods...!
so beautiful...cold...vacant...oft-times cruel.

Sob story

life is all too short and
there's so much to do. i'll
never finish my great epic
poem: SCUBA-DIVING FOR THE
HOLY GRAIL. not to mention my
SMELTING WORKS SYMPHONY. it's
all because of my humble orig-
ins and poor start in life. to
say i was slow off the blocks
is an understatement. my feet
are still somewhere in the peat
bog. it's no joke trying to
make it in the art worlds with
a head full of rubber termites
and monkey-tail dusters. my
latest poem is a protest called
DEVIL SPIT. it was murderously
castigated by the crits and my
tears of frustration were so
prolific they caused an ecological disaster and destroyed
all the strangler figs in the
rain forests. my next poem
will be called: MANGROVE UPPER-
CUT MY PROSTATES. and already

it's giving me the migraines.
life these days is really and
truly the slops. i feel like a
lone tiddler looking for a wife
and hungering for sweetmeats
in a muddy lake spiked with lysol
strychnine and prussic acid. hell
was never like this if my memory serves me right i actually
wrote a poem called: HAIL TO THE
NEW JERUSALEM AND THE BAILIFFS.

Rites of passage

yes i'm the bookworm
the one with the tired eyes.
no. i never said i was intelligent.
my mind if you want to know
is a truly magnificent
emporium of trash.
what's more i'm a corpse
and i take it i'm speaking
to Rent-a-Tomb and Cremation.
listen.   i'm in the early stages of
                              putrescence
so i can't afford to hang around.
no sales talk please
no elaborate confectionery
or you'll lose me to Paupers Graves.
already i'm giving off a grisly stench
like a marathon runner's shoes
marinated in farmyard urine.
no i don't want flowers
i don't want a solemn mass
i don't want a eulogy.
you'll be asking me next
if i want an amorous overture.
okay i'm being rude and distasteful
nothing personal i assure you –

put it down to inexperience, a certain rawness.
i only want to be bundled out of sight
in a place hermetically sealed
or burnt to ashes
if it's cheaper.
look. maybe i've not made myself clear
this has nothing to do with
personal vanity
it's a simple ecological imperative.
the least you could do
is send around the fumigation squad.

Conversation with god

i was having my usual morning
conversation with god. and this
time he wasn't mincing words.

i never interfere in human affairs
he said. i allow all you bastards
to get on with your own business
for good or for ill. it's no concern
of mine. if your nefarious doings bring bad
shit down on your heads, don't
blame me. i'm not calling the shots.

god, i replied, Wagner on the stereo
last night had me swooning
and levitating and my tape deck dropped dead.

is theology on the agenda today ?
god asked.

if you cut out the bunkum, i said.
some theologies are made of shrubs.
others are made of tall pine forests.
but your theologies are cabbage
patches and little gravel pathways.

you're assuming that i exist, said
god. you don't understand the paradox
of transcendence. you try to impose
conditions on the unconditional.

there are more holes in your metaphysics
i said, than faulty condoms coming
off the production lines.

you're a stupid old tosser, said god.
you should have been a bishop in a
diocese populated by anthropoids.

now that's what i call authentic, i
said. i like it. it's right on my
wavelength. keep that channel open
and there's a chance you'll win me
over.

this is nauseating, said god. your
ingratiating tone disgusts me.

the hot gospellers under your cassock
i said, otherwise known as crablice,
are regarded as rare delicacies
by the Amazonian stinkbird.

Odds-on forever

year '43 a few miles
south of Salerno. Sun,
for september, surprisingly
fierce. a unit of
Pioneers on gravedigging
detail being briefed by
their O.C. in a tomato
field across the road
from us – when a string
of 88's cuts through them
toppling some like wooden
puppets and flinging some
like rag dolls and
smashing up a stack of
packed and ready-for-market
tomato boxes abandoned
by the locals. we all
dive for cover, except
two guys, the quietest in
our outfit, who dash to
help the injured and shout
for stretchers and a truck
to get them to the M.D.S.
there are some men with
such strange disregard for

themselves, you simply
couldn't bet that they'll
live long. but the image
they plant in your mind
is an odds-on forever. I
can still bring their faces
clearly before me. I can
think of no reason why
they should remember mine.

A sort of life

my parent's voices are sleepwalking
in cosmology.
What they're trying to prove
I don't know.
They were always a mystery to me.
Back in the good old days
when we lived on faggots and peas
and my underpants were
constantly buffeted by flatulence
they my parents
would take me for walks in the
country.
They told me to listen to the daisies
sneering at the dandelions –
but all I could hear
were the earthworms
the high-voltages juices of
existential angst
crackling in their brains.
My father said, take him to the
doctor.
My mother said, doctors?
What do they know about the soul?
What that kid needs is a priest
an exorcist.

I completely lost my cool.
I threw my mother's rosary in the cesspit
and tore up my father's cabbage
patch.
He worked me over scientifically
with his razor strop.
Ever since then i've been convinced
that I have a problem
but with so many problems going
round
I can't decide which one it is.

Tinnitus

It was during the time of the bells
And female voices rasping be quiet be still
I learned to pray to Jesus.

He rode as I recall on a donkey
With a forehead hard and tuneless
as a treestump. Enviously I
Would think of this guileless animal
With his skull so unresonant, calm
And oblivious of the load of trouble
On his back. For I was
Afflicted with ringing in my ears,
And sleep had to compete with
The noises of a blacksmith shop.

And I prayed regularly to Jesus
To stuff my head with sawdust.

Dreaming and waking

Oz is over the rainbow
where the wardrobe is.   moths
and termites are expected.   don't
paddle in a steam of fear
and mooing.   cut the lawn.   you
may hear a cry from
the heart which is strangled
by a thread.   the tomcat is
motionless, peeing on the mint
that grows large for the roast
lamb, portending a juicy love
affair. a crow is Ivan the
Terrible. King Solomon was a
dark star for five seconds to
the billion years geological.
suck-ass artists may as well
sit on an egg as try to paint
the rainbow – but OZ is over it
somewhere, its Oscars throbbing
like bouncer's testicles
fighting off the alien jack-
the-lads who only want to join
the party.   there's no justice
in the world.   we're so surprised.

I'm the modernist poet

i'm the modernist poet.
as i cosh a huge blowfly
with a copy of the Golden Treasury
i repeat i'm the modernist poet

i'm the modernist poet. i take
a dazzling supernova
and wrap it in a mudpack of irony.

i'm the modernist poet. i subscribe
to the asymmetric principle.
the sound or sight of
regular metre and rhyme
is enough to curdle my face.

the beauty and truth business
gives me severe constipation.

romantic music is
like two fingers down my throat.
this morning – damn the radio –
i vomited violently on hearing
Respighi's Pastorale for
violin and string orchestra.

i'm the poet who abhors the poetic.
i'm the poet who epitomises
the self-lacerating paradox
of being an anti-poetic poet.

i'm the poet who's a grin-mix
of agony and belligerence
my beer gut magnificently mocking
my so-called artistic calling.

Poem with introduction

you don't have to read this
poem from beginning to end.
you don't have to read this
poem at all if you don't want to.
you are not asked
to do that. You do not
need to do that.

this poem is about pain.
If you've got this far this
poem is about pain and
everybody knows everything
there is to know about pain.

what can I add then? well
in my opinion pain has
an attitude I cannot – much
as I may try – concur with.

masochists are lucky people
if they are as reputed
able to transmute pain into
pleasure. which is something
I can't do, much to my regret.

pain then is nice for masochists
and I envy them I must say.
For if pain can intensify pleasure
there's at least a flicker
of light in pain's dark portfolio.

you need not have read this poem
but if you have and you're a
wretched moralist, I hope it has
intensified the pain of your
stupid problem. natter natter.
natter natter natter natter natter.

yes. from now on, natter natter.
and no more hauling the English
language around
like a blinding headache.

what i mean by what i say
before i say it

what i mean is:
my hinges have started to creak.
my body has become
a burial ground of muscle
and a breeding ground of flab.

what I mean is:
when I see grandeur
I see a holocaust looming up behind it –

but when I look back 70 years
what i see is
all just a fleeting commotion.

What I see is
reality jampacked with with emptiness –

by which I mean out there

I mean looking up out there
what I see is:
an incoherent windbag we call the universe.

What I mean is this:

how it is
is
we're all advancing backwards –
yet still we make a virtue
of consistency.

assuming an air of mock discourse
what I mean is:
only our breaths
truly intermingle and become as one –
the breaths from our mouths
and the breaths from our arseholes.

what I mean is:
we don't need a salvo of trumpets.
It only takes a single-barrelled fart
to demolish the spirit of seriousness.

what I really mean is this:
though we don't have wings, we can fly.
we each have the means of jet propulsion –
but we can only fly
    with true joy and freedom
when we untie the knot of self-importance
and let the air out of our balloons.

Little things

anyone may yet
live to regret
getting a life
or maybe not
it's all written
in our atoms
sniped atoms
pulverised atoms
epic and
teased atoms
smudged atoms
sons and daughters
of embers of
atoms
bright blue sky
agog
at fullblown
atom embers
shaped like
the high polish
on a coffin
or
the veneer
that passes
for wisdom

Something about her

i bought her a white mouse
                              – white
mice the craze those days. she
kissed it. i hated it. so did her
mother, tossed it over the canal
skyward.
                    she – not her mother – was
light, swift, infuriating
                                    and
she had feet so pretty and alive, i
wanted to cage them and feed them
                              tickle-finger.
                                                but
suddenly everything came down
to a question of jackets and trousers
because i was losing shape, togged
                              out, as i was
in sorely bedevilled delusions, and
feeling like the end product of a
                    bogus
                              genealogy.
last I saw her, we were sitting on
the railings, staring into the canal
our thighs
almost touching. i was tongue-tied.

                    her mother
                              was
shouting time for bed
using her starched bosom as a megaphone.
                    i felt
                              suicidal
a week –
then the high voltage of pride kicked
in and i ignored her – and her mother –
forever after.

Neural exposure

Inevitable these
Voiceless stops and starts

These patterns of subverted meanings.

Sentiments of purity are
The most inane tribute

And past these features lie
The unreachable crafted
Insubstantial

The approximate fiction
Overlaying
The acutely incomprehensible.

The aura of the like-the-thing-itself
Listens like a crude caress
To all that is calm
Glacial and macabre

A vulgarly indulged sonority
Softens the light around
A collar-and-tied executive
Fresh from the dream factory

A day in the life of a rag doll

Congealing colours of dawn
 to dusk
Form a watermelon face
 with wet disarrayed ringlets
Rum incense billows
  among tremelo needles.

Spray of gossamer sermons
Ice quills
      silicon orchids
     and mad limpets.

A day structured
     like a torn dragnet.

And Monica

truth is
        what
is it about?
            it
can't be serious.
    do you
hear yourself talk
    like a
    summary
          of
all the world's
    missing parts?
we are all
too much
done to.
         we all
test positive
for mortality.
      lurking
always
on the brink.
    LIFE/DEATH
is that
an even break?

I went with
a prostitute
named Monica
                and I
noticed
she had a full set
of fingers and toes.

Homage to futility

stretching itself out of sight
the giant anaconda
swallows a phantom

the phantom is the source
of the wind's rage
forever immured
in the faraway
unfathomable
stillness.

Holy Mary
Mother of God
the twangs of your eyes
as they ricochet
off your mirages
resonate in my headbones

with such tricks
stratagems
chicaneries
and fabulous hoaxes

i'm driven to screwing
around in the dark

with quantum mechanics and
soiled paper napkin sculpture.

Jesus Christ
as a common exclamation
and icon
of open heart surgery

why do i toil like a slave
to articulate
so feeble a defiance ?

this is my body
this is my blood
do this or that
in forgetfulness of me.

Awakening

Our darkness, over which the sun drools
even as it would flay a bald dome.

Restored by a long convalescence, universal laughter
embraces this poverty, this aimless future, dry and
unseeded, since undefiled by hope.

So this our very own darkness riveted to a nerve which
is doomed eternally to grope for a mermaid's crotch

Yes, yes, of course, indubitably wedded to an obstinate
abstraction, our darkness, breathless as a feather
achieves its perfection through self-parody

Thus over centuries darkness becomes darker than dark
and more frivolous—

only lapsing once in a while to be spooked by our old
family photographs

No real place

That I may come to proportion.

An equivocating light
A haze
Sometimes appropriate
Sometimes incomprehensible.

The whole of creation
Tampered with
Deformed, deflected
Perverted –
Never subdued.

Have you not also
Piddled around
With unassailable phoniness

And plied with soggy words
A gluttonous transcendence ?

Assuming words can travel
To another place
Just as unreal
As these trees, these stones
These church bells –

And these ghosts.

Where in the world
Is this parish?

New directives

On an endless straight road
No turning or looking back
Everything the same
       for everyone forevermore
Nothing can be forgotten or amended
She will see only hell   its dry vastness
She goes accompanied by pure light
       and its unrelenting echoes
At first a gentle breeze brings us together
No words
Only numbers in our heads
Interminable laughter
Everyone nameless
Self-obliterating togetherness
       moving forward nowhere
The heartless heart
Hopeless and untroubled
Deaf to the heavens' pathetic murmurings
We are always ahead of what is
No-one ever forgives
Hands free
 only to pound
      a valley of mud and knead it
         into a deeper and deeper density
And the body shall stifle its spirit

And day will arrive
 like an empty lot
        with a deafening white shimmer
She will wrap it all in a simulated scowl
Let everyone clam up on everything
Everyone say nothing's happening
Let the crazy-paving of biographies
        be compacted into
        one smooth flagstone

Hazards of sunset

A hint of green in the sunset
And out of the rigmarole of changing
                                    shapes
On a twitching and grimacing horizon
Rises something resembling
A red and gold goblet –

Filled, one assumes, with
The wine of the Gods.

On occasions like these
For light relief one may invoke
The hop-skip-and-jump spirituality
                of life –

Or trace the nebulous contours
The crevices and crypts of poetic
        construction.

As it is, I'm sitting here, dozing
And trying not to regret
Past voices I've condemned to silence,

When the melody I've been drifting on
Is suddenly awash with sad cadences

Tinged with the doleful inertia of
    eternity.

My head lolls back, and the
First unstoppable tear trickles over
The crest of my right cheek.

Autumn in july

I told her
she would have to choose
between me and the cosmos
She threw herself into
a spectacular identity crisis
Rancorous avant-garde music
was smashing up the radio
a time long gone
and still going forward
Our presumptuous westernisation
of the Yin and Yang
and how we would teach wolves
not to eat lambs
Marginal stuff like that
and more familiar things
that also take a delight
in telling us nothing.
Now into the fast lane
through the graveyard
Veer left at devil's takeaway
75 degrees
Enter the Red Dragon Inn
8.30 p.m.
Exit 11.50 p.m.
with a certain laxity of deportment

and the deviant imagination
yack-yacking to itself its plan
to write a definitive history
of Sealing Letters With a Kiss
           In autumn
when the leaves and petals
are breaking free
and – fools that we often are –
we say they are falling

Sub-texts

Suddenly I drop dead
Crash Down on her ribs
Lob your eyes out the window
Over the trees
You'll see a cloud shaped like a roach
My nightmares are blatant rip-offs
From Kafka's parables

Savagely chopping an onion
She is singing Therefore
She is
Her optimism   Which she wears
Like a flouncy dress
Is a cry for help

Flossing her teeth
Her eyes in the wild blue yonder
How to get friendly with gorillas
She often stitches a red carnation
To her ear

Go to hell   She says
But the thing is   I blurt out
You may be witnessing
My grandest nervous collapse

Or it could be senile decay

My doctor doesn't give a hoot
Chuckling to himself
He doodles day and night
Avalanche upon avalanche of pills

It hasn't been a great summer
Dizzy spells   Fat-free yogurt
Pains in the neck

But a thousand years ago
I visited the fabulous prostitutes
In Paris   Algiers   Naples
Rome   Milan   The Canaries
And the violins

The top & bottom of it

hark.
the poet sings
of love and hate and all the
other things and their
opposites
if only to palpate the dialectic
and administer
a wipe of rouge
to white and black magic
and smoke-puffs carousing in the whirlwind.
is he me, or am i he? i don't
know.
my pretence to authenticity
manoeuvring
to within a hairbreadths or as
good as a mile
of bigger-budgeted, reinspired
spin, if
only to comfort myself
in case i'm foredoomed to saint-
hood.
if this romance folds in
upon itself
so that nurses have to spoon
the drooping mouth and

change my nappies,
someone please drown me in cold
beer.
somewhere amidst everything
there's a dreamscape
disappearing into empty eye-
sockets.

Long ago but yesterday

All, but one, those days
Petals of forgetfulness.

A soft romantic haze
Caressing and soothing
The sun's fierce heat.

I think of a field
Full of moondaisies
So long ago and so near –

The joyous pillaging
That went on there.

As I harvested
The abundant, throat-high
Gold and white flowers

Who was the girl
The girl who called my name

Intoning it
Like a rare orchid?

Evensong

the light slinks away.
dreams ossify. solemn
perfumes excuse them-
selves. i scratch my
right ear with my left
hand and wonder. how
much idleness does it
take to create a world ?
lost ones. only you can
tell me why my eyes are
stewpots of boiling lava.
but i challenge you
to point to anything that's
not absurd. we'll talk
about our ruination when
our eyes are devious and
cryptic again with alcohol
and our faces have regained
their tactical flair. hands
hairs. tongues. how strange
and then the fiesta of
death grows tedious. there's
a halo around my feet. it
was forged in the Devil's
foundry. don't be surprised

if yesterday comes after
tomorrow. light a candle.
watch the flame lick the
silence. maybe the wax tower
weeps for joy at growing
smaller. a dog's howl is
begging for a fix and all
the pharmacies are closed.

Eloquently lost

Little woman of the cancelled mouth
Why so surprised and alarmed
That we're totally lost in this jungle?

Why so dismayed at not finding
Any unblemished roses in the archives?

Don't you know there's an education
In every nook and cranny –
At every step and turn an education

Much of which elevates and much
That degrades us – but you'll find
No unblemished roses in the archives?

Little woman with the strangled tongue
How natural it is that we're lost
And how strange it is that we should meet
In this vast and maze-like cathedral.

Little woman bereft of voice –
Beneath us (don't you know?)
There's one vault full of treasure
And another vault full of worms

And in each of them there lurks madness.

Little woman – so clearly surprised –
We're not just irretrievably lost,
But uniquely existent, each to each
As a strange and optional syllabus.

And much there may be to discover.

But no unblemished roses in the archives
Nor in any tolerable future.

Call me a liar

October sunsets can be so fast
As to render virtually meaningless
The concept of photographic memory.

This sunset began as a river of blood
That swiftly evaporated in a soft pink
Haze.

The haze turned light blue and
Through it emerged a charcoal
Grey eyepatch hemstitched with
greenish yellow thread.

Suddenly the eyepatch moved off
And accelerated at a terrific speed
to disappear like a UFO.

Immediately a luxurious black velvet
Cape was thrown with a great flourish
Across the north to south shoulders
of the horizon.

While all this was going on, I was
Being badmouthed by local moronic
Louts, creeps, psychos, primaeval

Screams, scumbags, scumbled copy-
Cats who hang out around the local
Takeaway.

Miraculously I managed to ignore them.

That's how it was. Call me a liar
If you like. It's too late now
To check it out anyway.

More to come. Very soon the black
Cape was having sequins stuck on it.

Joker

remembering the charm and stoicism
of the small terraces.
remembering, too, your breath, its
magically corrupt perfume
feathering my face.
i deluded myself into believing
your nearness was all i desired –
while your breast warmed to a hand
far bolder than mine.
and now (my defences
more sophisticated and alert)
when asked why i never married
i jokingly reply, oh that? well,
let me think, it was like this
most probably, what with one thing
and another, you know how it is,
there's always some small matter
that completely slips ones mind.

Disconnections

Five whiskies. Empty words.
The godforsaken edifice of your sighs.
This borough
In which I be domiciled
Is truly an hysterical one
Plus full bass percussion day and night.
Electronic acrimony.
Listen now
There's no reason whatsoever
To horse around with complex notions.
Eight whiskies and the global village
is the best joke going around.
Human endeavours make nine whiskies
And the rest is drizzle and drivel.
Since I never had the wit to disappear
I've had to settle for being
A cheap imitation of myself.

Like where's the end of a stream

They.
Who are they?
They are the Aldermen.
The zealots of law and order.
They have pacemakers.
They have cataracts.
They have pretty young wives
with social science degrees
psychology diplomas
and skillful ways with unmarried
mothers and their studs.

They have milked the sky –
the Aldermen.
And it so happens that
we all wake up every morning
miles apart from each other.

And have all the time in the world
to say nothing to our
situation.

And all that's familiar
with the sun
and old in the stone

and eternal in the superficial
sense as many breezes

all and all
have seen great battles swap
times and places –
seen famous warrior kings
sitting dumbly on stuffed ponies

and all
that's perished in the mud
along with old shrapnel-in-head grandpa
who once ate the leg of a
dog.

Directionless

Love is lost in the forest
Λ plaintive female cry
Coming from everywhere and nowhere
Filtered through centuries of
Illusion dampness rheumatism
None of which rules out
That it could be her very own Hiroshima
Eros is still too edgy
Torn between Genesis and putative
Biological intention
Never to encounter Titans
And Norse Gods
Bearded   yeasty and gross
Their dreary trudging old fugues
Vainly seeking an echo in the
Vast emptiness
Where earth and sky are joined
By invisible stitching

A kiss too late

The way it transpires is
The way fate touches
The way
A life-long predilection
Misleads
And when all my cool machinations
Are exposed after all the more
As no caprice of free will

There's a flaw destined
To be shadowed forever
By a teardrop's spectre

And kisses that never were
And words of love unuttered
And uttered too late
And a dead forehead kissed
Like dry lips on parchment.

The way it transpired was
The way regrets grow
Like mildew on old snapshots
That are kept in damp seclusion

Like affections locked up, damned

In their own perspiration
And sealed by an
Unrecognisable pain.

And now these leakages
Unforeseen, uncontrollable
And a locket I dare not open.

Vapour trails

You were never really here
Shrub
Did you want to be tangible like grass ?
You were too brittle   Lacked resilience
The earth drinks its own sweat
Is an eater of fire

Salt
On the adolescent's eyelids
A wet dream is made   His mother
Washes the bedsheets
Says nothing   She's still puzzling
Over how she conceived the brat
When she had a headache for a year

And where did he learn his bad language ?

A summer day in a slow swoon
So much succulent flesh flowering
Deep O deep are the lies
From the catacombs of impeccable grammar

Children grow up
To despise their over-anxious parents
And do their jungle stuff

In old warehouses

For it has to be ceaselessly argued
That humanity will prevail

Though even
From the shallowest dawn there rises a mist
That will never be grasped in our hands
Nor in our heads

Aphorisms

every second
is adjacent
to a second second.

every day is a dice
suing for importance.

every clarification
has the hauteur
of sour mayonnaise.

no words
can simulate
the bassline
of true emptiness.

there are sleeping nosebleeds
that resemble the smears
of passionate lipstick
on celibate pillows.

nicotine sickness
combined with a dead telephone
brings on brainwaves so feeble
they couldn't rock a cradle

in a doll's house.

demure hormones
timidly paging
vain expectations of valour.
well
what d'you expect?

no preponderance
of indifference
that doesn't have its star raconteur.

evasions
prolongations of evasions
are pensive ragamuffins
scaling the Himalayas
of disintegration.

Approximately hereabouts

ring-a-roses
on shoes of snow
the wind fractious
from scrubbing icebergs

and down Maytree Close
garden flats
an old wilting dragon
cloning the pixies

i avail myself of a weed
legs go sailing
cares rock blithely
on their beam ends

ace falls to jackass

i once had
two entire grandmas
built like stevedores

i chased them
round the ludo board
stunned them
with a septic finger

they never came to

i'm afraid

nobody was puzzled
the cheese crumbled
in the mousetraps

lost photographs
faded photographs

you planned everything
my cheap little kodak

Words of wisdom

the corner shop is okay
                              but
it gets confused when
            pricing oddments
such as
stray drinking straws and
rotting bananas.

                  overfed
tabbycats befog us
            and even
            if our eyes mutate –
God (it must be said)
never promised to be fair.

                              nor
did those who prop him up.
Matt. Mark. Luke. Jack.
Richard the Lionheart,
                  Rasputin
and all the dear old pious
hanging judges.
                  nuns and
total noses toast dirty totem
poles

and give little
boys bottoms
a whack.

asleep. we
are most times asleep

while
the saliva tycoons spit on
everything
and send out
their final demands.

tubas AND
mumps can numb your harps
and undermine your molars.

say a prayer when
you push out your punt.

Cider house binge

I know he's a bastard, said Flo.
Nice guys are okay for some
But not this bitch – get me?

I'm listening, I said. And I
Bought her a sadistic treble vodka
Because i knew it would paralyse her tongue
And take her legs away.

It was the night Robin Hood
Forgot his mackintosh.
So we all got drunk, singing, hugging
Quarrelling and having psycho-
Analytical encounters.

The wall-mounted stag's heads
Were smoking superkings, wearing baseball caps
Smirking, soliciting an excessive
Amount of attention –

To wind up the jealous little dogs
Render them hysterical, bust their
stupid throats, collapse them – the
full payback.

On its way down to the floor
Flo's face struck the edge of a table.
She lost a front tooth, spat blood
Into a pool of beer, cider and glass –
And her lips came up like two sausage balloons.

I moved to assist her – but her hardman
Shoved me aside. I said, she's all yours.
You see, it's like this: I'm a really
Nice guy, polite, gentle, generous and
Terribly romantic.

Ordinary bleeding

I stared at the girl
She was very chestnut
She stared back clearly
Could commit murder.
Sorry I'd scared myself
I looked beyond her
Hoping for a scene of
Order on some backcloth
An appearance, say, of
A booklined sitting room
An impossible comfort
In the circumstances.
After all, this was
Not a stage set.
I was not dreaming
Not daydreaming not
Any kind of dreaming
I've ever known. I
Returned my gaze to
Her. She led me into
A room, unlike any
Room I'd seen. It was
Blood-drenched, floor
To ceiling. I felt
No horror, no sense of

Repulsion. No gratitude
No sense of duty. Nothing.
And for the first time
Realised: I'd always
Known that bleeding is
A very ordinary and
Innocent business.

Going to pieces in the launderette

She came in carrying her laundry
in a black binliner.
Her skin stark white, offset
by all-black mini skirt
nan's shirt, high heels, hair
and eyes.

I say hello. nice mornin'.
Everything's working okay.
No screaming parts, no cracked
bearings, no death rattle. I'm
harmless really, though I bear
the stigmata of the
indisputable bronchitis.

But I mustn't distract her
as she feeds the machine with
her fancy underwear, bed linen
gloriously stained and fragrant
from a serious week-end's fucking.

I'm scratching my left forearm
down to a fleabite's core.
I'm standing by a tree.
I'm looking at a muddy river.

I'm kicking a stone.
I'm looking for a pathway
of mysterious warp, deep intrigue.

I'm lost in a forest of cold eyes
ponderous ghosts
whispering exorcists, hangovers.

I stick two thousand years
of philosophy together, so that
they form a heavy solid object
with which to clobber a giant
man-eating crow
walking slowly towards me.

A significant day in the life of a third-rate consumer

a once familiar street, but
the houses had all shrunk and
huddled together.
they found me repugnant, i guess,
because i owned nothing, had
no property rights.

i was flushed, incongruous, tensely
surpressing giggles
as i often had to do when a child
queueing up for holy communion.

mirthful voices, sighs of melancholy,
abrasive, pan-scrubbing noises
resounded in my head
as if it were a Victorian kitchen.

I was hungry and dying to relieve
my bladder; grinning involuntarily
as i looked around for a public
convenience, which i knew i would
never find in a thousand years.

Then i remembered: a currant bun

in my pocket. As i bit a huge chunk
out of it, i could feel eyes and
ears everywhere.

what's the problem? i shouted.
doesn't a guy have the right to
consume a currant bun in these parts?
or is he only allowed to partake
of the body and blood of Christ?

The lace-curtains were doing a merry
dance. And, as i sank to my knees
in a pool of my own urine, i felt
a new chill in the air and heard
the wail of sirens getting louder.

Naughty boy

It was just after morning prayers
in the local cider house.
I was leaning on the bar when
this guy sidled up to me.
You're a nutter, he said.
Watch it, I said, you're dabbling
in classified material.
A thousand immensities will descend
on the whistle-blower.
You're the sort of nutcase, he said
who needs a big cock up his ass.
Do you think that would do the trick
I said, like sorta straighten me out?
How did you escape from the bin?
he said.
The tambourine man was in cahoots
with the turnkey, I said, and we tossed
a brown envelope into the monkey circus.
You trying to be funny? he said.
Languid, sonorous adagios, I said
sudden strident crescendos
Beethoven boiling over, Napolean
scratching his piles, the jackal's howl
and the moon hating us all.
I looked in the mirror, my face split

in two by a bottle of red wine – an
awful bloody cloven grin.
Maybe he's right, I thought. And turned
to congratulate him on his insight.
But he was gone.
The jukebox was thudding, the barmaid
was screaming at a spider.
Hit it with your pussy duster, I shouted
and measure me a double scotch. I'm
depressed and hallucinating and I can't
get it up these days.
Behave yourself, she said, or I'll
give you the cane.
Just what I need, I said. As I worked
on a fat roll-up of dangerous substances
otherwise known as good shit.

Two renegades smoking weird cheroots

They were praying in the morning sun
When suddenly one said to the other
I can't stand this bullshit
This twisted experiment by God.
All he does is dish me bleak, trendy postcards
Via the sweatshop called Royal Mail.
Hell, I'm thinking of selling out to praxis
Like viagra bust my balls
After dawn-to-dusk working hours
At peak performance level.
Then the other said to the one
I've had it with your paradox sandwiches
And intellectual Molotov cocktails
They screw me up and make me point beyond myself
As a figuration of flickering cadences
A woefully deficient strategy of hibernation.
God was a month short of his ten-thousandth birthday
And was already popping psilocybin and speed
As he wandered down T.S. Eliot's Rats Alley
Looking for a postbox.
Bastards, he said, they don't know nothing yet.
I've got my reputation to protect.
From now on it's prussic acid, strychnine
Oil slicks, fifty-mile tailbacks, nuclear holocaust.

And if that doesn't tickle their fancy
They get soaps twenty-four hours daily, all channels.

The dump

Nightime moonlight it's cold
And God looks down from above
Sitting on top of this dump
All his millions of loveless nights
Alas, sleepless nights as well
Up there on top of the dump.

It's cold, but apart from that
It's relatively peaceful down here
This little corner of England
So far from the world's turmoil.

All quiet and peaceful down here
At least til the splendour of dawn
When the sun shall rise, spitting fire
And poison and God knows what.

This little poem, then, for God
Up there in his overrated glory –
Though he and I are not really friends
Nor exactly enemies either.
It's simply my humble opinion
That God should dump this dump.

The poetry circle

of the time we were a bunch of creeps.
we sat in a circle
doing nothing creepy in the
darker meaning of the term
though creeps we certainly were.

poems were what we wrote but did we
write something?
that's a question we evaded
by discussing it
with a flurry of soft blows to the
rhyming couplet
and savagely skinning peanuts.

baloney said someone we're nothing more
than a gap between commercials.

that's a smartass line said someone
else
where-as and however and in truth
a gap is where a woman extradites
a guy
from uptight trousers and gives him
joy and release.

in the truer way of truth
what we most craved was flattery.
flattery palpates the cortex
and brings you out in a charismatic rash
resembling pukey tattoos
or vanity publications.

no one wrote a poem entitled: COOL SHIT
REIGNS SUPREME IN THE CIDER HOUSE.
but someone bravely recited one
about the grey blizzards of permanent winter
and getting it off
in a council towerblock elevator
while standing in a pool of urine.

and we've never been sober since.
nor have we been drunk.
nor does anything make sense
or nonsense.
nor is anything true or false.
nor did we really exist or not exist.

One fatal flaw

splitting the atom
by psychokinesis.
doing a grand tour
of the solar system
in my anti-gravitational luxury cruiser.
instituting licenced brothels
for all sexes.
re-opening the Garden of Eden
reinstating Adam and Eve
along with the tree of knowledge
and the kindly old serpent.
knocking up against the Aussies
the fastest double-century on record.
winning four Olympic golds.
masturbating in public
with dazzling style and panache.
horsewhipping the parliamentary whips.
banning for all time
the Last Night of the Proms
and just for an extra kick
abolishing Tchaikovsky's
piano concerto number one.
no sweat.
all in a week's work.
revising my surrealist poem PICKLED ONIONS

revision upon revision
each one more prosaic than the one before.
conceding defeat to the muse.
utterly deflated. dishonoured.
nothing for it but to slink away
and blow my brains out.

Shopping list

olive oil, meat, toilet rolls.
yes, ignore the ink, your handprints
that left the tap running
drawing the darkness down
to sagging floorboards.
coffee, million memories, loss of control.
and there it was
dying in the moss or fungus
starved, blind – the stillness holding
on to, washing up liquid, biscuits, honey.
suddenly, in the damp cellar
unutterable zeros oriented on their own
circularity.
no heavy gimmicks, only derided sinews
unwinding from your forehead, as all
the nothing that we are
rears up, proudly homeless, on
spectacular polysyllabic bravura.
rice pudding, tin soups, salami or
garlic sausage, street footsteps, where
waste girls' wombs were wasted.
then come tears like weak beer
and night milks the groans
of candlewax kiss, torn roses, insomnia
alphabet noodles or spaghetti loveletters.

Dogmas cover the world like glass domes

dogmas cover the world like glass domes.
if you've got a hole in the head that's
lusting for a diamond stud you'd better
get to heaven be safe.
i do not know weather spices are funny or
serious smelling as they do of new-wave
solemnity and atonals being bandied around
like wax-fruit platitudes.
we swirl around in our multi-coloured whirlpools
of escape.
we don't understand.
we understand nothing. why not. we
don't understand. ah yes. and most of us
will never share a bed with each other.
does it matter.
does it matter that there's been
a fusillade of cosmic mayhem just for this?
no. it doesn't matter. it doesn't.
i wish i could stop.
i wish i could just shut up.
i'd be happy just to stay silent if i could
but it's difficult it's impossible
as difficult as blowing in my own ear.
we need to be sharper. not sharper like in

sharp practice. but sharper like in
watch the birdie. though sometimes
i wish i could be duller and once and for all
time simply shut my trap.
dogmas cover the earth like glass domes.

Partly this partly that

Inspired by surveillance fantasies
we're all in excellent shape
and well-adjusted to the universe
as it grinds away on its way
to another Christmas.
  Is anyone bewildered? Hear this:
bewilderment is sexy
especially as a slogan on a virginal
or otherwise intense white t-shirt.
BEWILDERMENT IS SEXY. Are you
thinking of murder? Be assured
(even if you are serious) your thoughts
can't be read by the cameras
unless you're trapped
in a 1950s movie.
  Me and my imaginary sweetheart
are freaky funpacks
we write each other barcode poems
more cryptic than the love letters
disguised as greasy stains on doors.
  Of course we're all bent.
Bored sometimes but mainly bent.
Some of us bend the way the world bends
others the other way.
Same difference. We're all suckers

perfectly lined up for the ultimate curve-ball...

Kangaroo head

there will come a vast psychic night
when all we'll hear is the throbbing
of the kangaroo head.

the primal scream of the cosmos
the droning insomniac propellors of the moon
we'll remember as heavenly music
compared to the phallic throbbing
of the kangaroo head.

we who have unwillingly issued
from what's knows as normal copulation

we who have persistently sanitised
all physics all poetry all magic

we with our fine sensibilities
we with our hypocritical pleasantries

will learn what it's like to be
buggered by the kangaroo head.

for we are nothing more than abominations
to the kangaroo head.

may God have mercy on us.
swarming horrors though we are
what have we done to deserve
the curse of the kangaroo head
while other vermin go free and unaware?

ask no more questions. for questions
only serve as incitements
to the murderous lust of the kangaroo head.

All talk grub tub

Sweet potatoes, says old Bungalow,
Boiled in their jacks.
Fighting mad cockerel, i say
Bled, plucked and drawn by young virgins,
Lightly blowtorched, slowly roasted.

Bugs and worms slosh and squabble
In the wet grass. And how
The dead do rant at the rocky crags.

A delirium potential in everything
Bewith and beyond cranky doodles
Oceans of bedevilled cosmics
Gutted suckers, trundle-cups.

Moonglow stains on black trousers.
Eyes like pancake mix
Shot with wild beetroot relish
Faggy woes, drool, dread, forgotten jokes.

Old Bungalow is asleep
Tired out trying to get a word in.

The time is what is now how
The revulsion routine rehashes

Serious talk with trite asshole dazzle
Till all that's left is rabbit crack-up
With cold fries in remote grottoes.

Tracey Emin's bedroom

And the lady said:
Sex became a bowl of grits
something to tamp down the paranoid
overlaps
when existence karate-chops you
into peddling your snatch
for small change.
     And she paused. Then continued:
Net loss, net gain:
Scatbrain and scutgut, punctuated
by doleful cadences, bulimia
with pizza binges, the skulking smirks
sweats, shivers, palpitations.
A carpet of used tampons
breeding maggots.
Mocking laughter echoing round the walls.
     Taking a chance on fresh air
I see Jesus Christ
spreadeagled on a busy crossroads
wondering why he got kicked out
of clubland
and how he might cut the mustard
in a kindlier light.
     Are you still alive? There's
many a bizarre twist on that one.

It takes a weird sense of humour
to permit the world to exist.
    Dinner is served.
Fierce.

On the joys of being sexually inactive

i'll never get it right. i'll
never get the right itch
on these thoughts. they
don't seem to understand
themselves.
              it's all because
the world
is full of everybody fucking.
the manifesto of fucking
is splashed over everything.
don't get me wrong. i'd be
glad very glad were i too also
strenuously fucking. but i'm
not even feebly fucking.
why?
i'll come back to that
question later.
              but meanwhile
if i go on like i'm going
i'll forget what fucking means.
impossible
one might say.
but i forget nearly everything
else.
         so why shouldn't i

forget fucking?
　　　　　and here's a
joyous thought i might do well
to clutch onto:
　　　　　maybe if i for-
got fucking i would no longer
be bothered by the fact that
i'm the only person in the world
who is not fucking.
　　　　　anyway
i blame it all on transcendental
meditation. first i meditated on
cosmic mashed potato. then i switched
to meditating on
　a rasher of moon glow.
　　　　　you've
got to be ruthless in this world
and keep on going regardless.
　　　　　　but
my implacable determination on
transcending everything got me into
stopping fucking.
　　　　　i don't think i'll ever
get this or anything right.
　　　　　not
even in the cosmological solace
of my moments of levitation.

You'll know it when you hear it

i first heard it from a dead mule
it was lying on its back and its
body was so bloated that were it not
for its hooves you'd think it had
no legs. then i heard it from the
tail-half of a cockroach. i'd given
the thing such a kick i never found
where the half with the head went. i've
heard it from the sinuses of a very
nondescript portrait in oils. i've
heard it from sparrows trapped in
glass stairwells and knocking themselves senseless. heard it from huge
spiders in the bath and still heard
it after the plug closed them
down in the swirling water. i've
heard it from the fly-specks on the
lampshade just as i was thinking that
the boredom and apathy would never
end.

i've heard it from many things
many creatures alive and dead. you
name it i've probably heard it from
it. it's not useful information. it
can't be translated or described in

any known language – but that goes
for many books also and the noises that
issue from the mouths of pundits and
so-called learned men. i doubt whether
god himself has heard it. he doesn't
listen to anyone or anything as far as
i can make out. you must hear it if
you haven't already you must hear it
for yourself and you'll know it straight-
away – though like me or anyone you
won't be able to translate or describe
it.

      imagine chewing sand and washing it
down with sump-oil while your teeth are
rotting and your duodenum is being
steam-ironed and your eyeballs are
being sucked out through a straw. well
that's something but it's really nowhere near it.

      one can't just go on
saying what it's not. all i can say is
it's something like music of a kind one
has never heard before. you'll know it
when and…

Downers anytime

I don't know. i am what i am
because of more booze than sex
or being what i am
has driven me to
more booze than sex.
but I've given my
doctor strict instructions
never in any circumstances
put me on intensive care.
i've had my fill of intensity
and all it's done
is wreck my nervous system.

give me a downer anytime
and if things become critical
turn me into a cabbage.
a cabbage is absolutely brain-dead
is what i mean what i mean is
i've never seen a cabbage look unhappy
I've never seen a cabbage
that looked like it needed anything.

we are liars and self-deceivers
hypocrites
over-excited fools.

we call each other couch potatoes
if we watch too much teevee.

bullshit. cant. humbug.
a genuine couch potato
will sit all day and night
watching nothing registering nothing
while its innards decompose
and its skin slowly shrivels
and sprouts fatuous little penises.

Long nights

Lucky if sleep brings
Dreams so full
Of twaddle and chaos
They astonish and alarm
The very stars.
If there's no lust
To hug
Be dada be dada
Be damned
The dust dies downhill
And the world's stink
Rises forever
Ever wherever it's going.
And sometimes
Black girders of thought
From the scaffolding
Of long nights.
So come on over, friend
Friend from
Friend from friend
Friend from
The gullies of your insomnia.
Sigh
Seek
Think a thought

Definitely
Think a thought
Sprawl and speak
or listen like a lizard
Til the horizon
Is smeared
With the first signs of dawn.
We are children
Of the salt dew
Cities flames cities spew.
It's not our task to hold
The universe together.

Too late for a glamorous death

death? don't talk to me about death
i've had it up to here with the whole business
i've died many times in many places
a hundred maybe a thousand deaths
but i've never died in an armoured vehicle
hit by a missile exploding in a fireball
and flying apart in upwardly mobile fragments.
all my deaths have been well structured
like the winners of major poetry competitions
deaths in the dull orthodox soporific mode.
often i've wandered about death's funfair
wearing my HIT ME WITH A FIREBALL t-shirt
but it seems i lack what it takes
to turn a fireball on or even cop a bullet
it's as futile as wearing a KISS ME QUICK hat
and expecting a juicy smacker from Miss Universe.
whenever i go walking
down the throat of the city
where the foul gasses blowing two ways
cause the rain to crosshatch
the whole frenetic scenario
and the glitzy happiness bubbles
bubble so brightly the bubbly little fuckers
unperturbed by my sullen hangover face
as i proceed flip flop flip flop

down the belching gullet of the overfed city
with my suicidal morning-after demeanour
i defy all the red lights
deliberately to court my spectacular demise
get a vehicle to toss me in the air
like a graceful and celebrated matador
meeting his glamorous fate in the bullring –
but the traffic always slows down
  to let me across safely
while the drivers eye me with pity and contempt
as one who's totally devoid of grace and panache
and would certainly die a most ungainly death.
so that's another sad fact i must endure
i've come to resemble a stupid old fart
too pathetic even to provoke
the hair-trigger rage of the driving fraternity.

God is dead and the devil is shagged out

Parents are monsters
Once upon a time I'm a virgin again
How cutely the snowflakes dither
And what's her majesty's flag
Doing on the church tower?
Cast my seed on her cornflakes
Set the mange on her poodles
I love my little rebellions
The spectre of my nose
All aglow with murder by telepathy
If I ruled the world
Tootsie goodbye
All things bright and beautiful
And fatso doing the Puccini
Deep O deep
Is the great ocean of semantics
Swedish Bitches on the buzzer
Quick Relief Raving Nymphs
And other angels of mercy
Winding up the hellfire preachers
Old Nick
Is a friend too late
Busting his balls not for nothing
In vain all the same

I got you babe on the shopping list
With tissues and clingfilm
Pharmaceutical survival kits
Meatballs in Bolognese
All sorts of stress-related goodies
Alongside the checkout
Can't go wrong
When this sweet rage grips my guts

Another zeitgeist ago

I sat halfup
Rested my right elbow
On your right cheek.
You stopped breathing for a while.
Then, just as I began to wonder
If I should be worried, you started
Breathing again, with a terrible rumpus
In my armpit.
Long, very long, ago.
You won't remember. More probably
You were asleep
Beating up and strangling your teddybears.
I flew in a boot.
People could scoff, but then,
Neither had we heard the music of Stockhausen.
You snorted, turned over, your back to me
And you said, Damn bonk sagging wingnuts.
A certain haughtiness
Or indifference
Opened up a distance between us that seemed
To mock my manhood.
I tried to clarify the Zeitgeist.
But something about my philosophy
In those days was like soggy quartermoons
To the Japanese.

Either that or it put their temples
In diapers.
I got up, groped around in the dark
Found the washbasin, lathered my face
with a used condom.
Can't recall exactly, though i swear to god
We were having a marvellous time
In the heat, the humidity
And among the mountains of cigarette butts.

Midnight oil and randy ballpens

treetops shivering. their waft droves
language tricks swirl like a woman's
hemline. do options cheat. have knack
of into heels enticing good soldiers
from holy communion. o come on, let us
all be gutter worthy flirters, hot and
eager in the matter, as when eyes make
their entrance with sunset martinis in
them. selfless shadows and strutting
scholars all, widowed by loneliness or
marriage. reassembled with tics added
and so far behind our future we are
already souvenirs buried under glossy
new gizmos. at least our eyes cocktails
have never been spiked by evil empires.
who crashes you, love? the mirrors mop
their brows, labouring under night's
tyranny – the fragrance of rutting pens.

Conversational leakages

with regard to your question
of the question of our being here
this inexplicable arrangement
of us, as you put it
and what does it all mean and such stuff
as if what something is
has got to mean something else.
no, of course i'm not blind.
i can see there's a lily
sprouting from your Japanese print
and i never said a word about hallucinations.
but how can you possibly know
that flowers are listening to everything
and detecting falseness and deception all around ?
okay. so you've been swept off your feet
by the muscular splendours
of Antonio.
but yesterday you said the same
about Larry Bossel's spiky hairdo.
and only last week
if i dare mention it
you were obviously wetting your knickers
at the mere sight of the gold ring
in Jason the Bongo's upper lip.
now what has any of this got to do

with what Jesus the crucified said ?
"i am the true vine."
if i've heard it once
i've heard it a thousand times
and it means, i suppose,
that the rest of us are common or garden brambles.
forgive me if i piss in your kitchen sink.
Harry Krishna. Who's he ? what's his ballgame ?
okay. go ahead. tell me all about him.
yes i'm listening. i'll listen
to anything you say.
it's bound to be less excruciating
than having my brains screwed by your Tarot cards.

Essay on symmetry

slap me hard on one cheek.
and just to straighten me up
slap me hard on the other cheek.
now i'll strip to the waist.

stick a knife in my solar-plexus.
stick an identical knife
in the small of my back.
now i'll bare my lovely bottom for you.

take a good stout cane
swing it with all your might
and make a horizontal red stripe
across each beautiful buttock.
now fuck me up the arse if you please
and i'll show you my naked feet.

i see you've got your jackboots on.
so you stamp down hard on my right foot
and stamp with equal force on the left foot.
now stand back – admire your work.
you've done a tidy and symmetrical job.

the Union Jack is symmetrical.
the swastika is symmetrical.

military parades are symmetrical.
the pillars and pediments
of the establishment are symmetrical.
the huge concrete office blocks
of bureaucracy and high finance
are symmetrical.
Victorian terraces of poverty
are neat, tight and symmetrical.

the ancient Greeks loved symmetry.
the Romans loved symmetry.
the Nazis loved symmetry.
their citadels and triumphal arches
were exemplars of symmetry.
and all three mighty empires
tumbled down in carnage and chaos.

there are three wooden crosses on Calvary
they stand very holy and symmetrical.
but the three victims nailed to them
look like as if they've had it
up to the eyeballs with holiness and symmetry.

incidentally
i too am thoroughly sick of symmetry.
and i've felt this way about it
long before you worked me symmetrically over.

Certain standard ravings of old age

For who snarls
There are no official guidelines
So it's down the bog with my love poems
They were all a crock of unction anyway
It only so happens it is Autumn
Much too early in the morning
Tears big as mistletoe berries
Attest to my complex nature
As I wake sobbing from a dream
Of bringing down a screaming diva
With a flying rugby tackle
There's a yellow scorpion in the marmalade
The doughnut of quiet countenance
Is easily confounded by fools
With garrulous entrails
Destiny calls
I must get my act together
It's going to be all go from now on
Pumping iron between cigarettes
Challenging the new millenium to a naked mud-fight
Sucking up to a bureaucrat's arse with my hoover
Dracula's daughter on the sex hotline
Promises to send me a D.I.Y. mag
So I'll be totally self-sufficient
And ruthless

New fangs
A fearsome wolf-whistle
A vitriolic pen
With which I'll write hate poems
To the bus company
And sign myself Cyber-Punk

Love poem

I'm just a sickening old hunk of
 tired flab
But my glands go into a swelter
 when you're around
The whole fabric of your suffering is
Indecent in its fragrant delicacy.
In the midst of the zombie-like mob
 mesmerised by videos
You spit forth with grace the poison
 of your charm
And when I start writing
 with decrepit fervour about you
All that comes out is
 psuedo post-modernist puke.

A slight technical problem

i ring her up to tell her i've
been busted for shoplifting. and
all she can say is please don't
bother me now because i'm busy on
my penis and testicles painting.

her astringently posh accent
always makes me feel insecure.
thus i've come to realise how
a potato chip must feel when
being doused with vinegar.

so i write to her. Dear Trish
allow me seriously to imagine
that your penis is depicted
marching down Kings Road dragging
its testicles behind it like a
sack of pumpkins.

                              or should i
imagine something snappier like
a penis and balls being proudly
displayed in the palm of your
favourite hunky bartender. or a
great dreadnought of a cock
running amok in a lesbian gym?

and by the way. does said penis
have a shadow? i ask because mine
hasn't got one. i've stood nude
in every pose and in strong light
from every angle. but i can't get
my penis to cast a shadow anywhere.

maybe my penis is a ghost despite
all the trouble it's gotten me into
since my adolescence. and that's
a very long time chronologically
so to speak – notwithstanding your
opinion that i haven't grown up yet.

Dinner party

due to a slight blunder
with a fish knife
a chicken's thighbone
flies across the room.

our hostess
she turns to me and says
excuse me she says.

sorry i say
i was making a leap of faith...

and you crashed the first fence
she says.

as always i say
it's the narcotics...

the days when everything
is nothing someone says...

are becoming more common
i say.

and now they're coming

in cult movie monochrome
our pretty hostess says.

a few more centuries
of grand scale atrocities
someone else says
and we'll have a perfect world.

and the sun-kissed sphynx
will disgorge sugar hearses
i say.

lipstick-on-penis expressionism
our ravishing hostess says.

and i don't care if it comes
with rough trade
and cheap perfume i say.

downwind of the table
a preacher is expounding
the great loaves and fishes scam.

blew all the gaskets
in the engine of market forces
the preacher says.

things were bound to turn ugly

our fabulous hostess says
as she passes me another joint.

How Jamie committed suicide as a protest against social integration

He picked up the telephone
dialled Samaritans.
As pertaining, he said, to this
so-called life, from which
I'll soon be opting out,
I hereby give notice
that I wish to say something obscene.
Stay on standby
you mealy-mouthed bastards.
Then he slammed the receiver down.

Starting from the top:
He had to store up a thousand pills
of varying sedative powers
while ostensibly hearing voices
and having a dangerous fling
with metaphysics.

Midst all this abundance
a certain guile notwithstanding
rude health and other disasters...

Something to do with microcosmosis

word processing, databasing,
networking, etcetera, and how
– if there was a way how –
to nullify the gaze of the other.

His funeral
was a long and tedious business.
Smothered in sprays and wreaths
and solemn platitudes and gazes
what could he do for revenge
but cynically give up the ghost ?

And what could he say
as a parting shot to the world
but this: what's there to be
sad and sorry about ? –
except that the hangovers
appear to have arrived before the binge.

Come to think of it, he added,
what the hell is all this ceremony
around this heap of shit called Jamie ?

Melancholic

Nobody understands
Clumps of stiffs they all are
they can't see what dallies in the sunset glow
and how tomorrow looks in askance
at the donkeys of Cairo choking in the traffic
Nobody understands
my heroic aspirations
my hiss my sheen my flaring matches
my ghost leaping from sleep
my fingers tapping
against the unbearable silences
Convention keeps us erect
though sometimes it would seem
We are remnants of some terrible accident
Nobody understands
why I hang a neo-pop strawberry vagina
on the wall
and put a brand new
summer-fresh polyester cover
on the sad sofa
Times I have worked my balls off
for peanuts makes me blush
and chase my thoughts away into the blue abyss
Hope reigns eternal
The world is waiting for the sunrise

Why ? I can't pretend to know
Maybe it's because Eve fellated the serpent
Nobody understands
why I sit down and draw little octagons.

In self-defence

Whenever you like, I said, I'm not going
anywhere. Quibbles and crumpled suits, okay ?
Them I threw his ginger snaps on the floor
and stamped on them.
This is my prayer: kick my butt but let no
blood be spilled. And may it please God to
cure me of snorting correction fluid.
The wasp stings with malice aforethought. But
I'm a fool. Always was. Always will be. So
I don't have a clue as to why I do anything.
Get it ?
Weekdays I eat dirt. Sundays I eat newspaper
cuttings. Every day I drink the very dregs of
the trickle-down of affluence.
Can't get a bit of skirt for love nor money nor
swastikas.
Could be why I write poems that make me tremble
and turn pale, sorta putty-like, and run a
dangerously high temperature. Who knows ?
Sceptics in all your glory, can't you see I'm
not fooling ? I'm a *genuine* fool.
You'll be making a grievous mistake if you
regard me as a common rib-nudging joker.
Thank you.
I dream every night a new twist on the last

tango. And I wake up every morning in the same old rancid sweat, to resume my search for the truth. I rest my case.

My latest book

of all my poems i love
my signature best it has
such chilly fluidity and
such variations of
slant it's an artworks
in itself and my rare
and pallid silences are
more sublimely ambiguous
than my poems i've pub-
lished my latest hard-
back of a hundred blank
pages with only my si-
gnature on and people
ask me to sign it and i
say that's a hundred and
one they say i'm the gr-
eatest then i read my no
book in clubs with those
spectral acoustics and
dim light of candles in
wine bottles and the aud-
ience bangs the tables
and shouts crap bullshit
and gedoff but you got
to keep a serious face

cos poetry is serious ai-
n't it what with people mad drunk and waiting for
the jazz group to come on
i'm such a lucky bloke an
i ain't got lynched yet.

How he did jig

he won a shop

when everyone said oh ah
oh ah oh ah
he won a tent

                then he told
                ten wry lies
                and poured
                his leg
                into dry ice

he said eee war pee
and oh hell a rupee
in the rubble

           then he
           bought himself
           a pet gnu

                a gnu
is a creature that costs a lot of
tin
it is very ribald
and active
and has

absolutely no veneer

but what was he doing
in Skye

Putting the record straight

I've never written a poem
called KNUCKLEBONES.
I know it seems crazy
to have to publish
this denial
but
everywhere I go I get
accused of
or complimented on
being the author
of some poem entitled
KNUCKLEBONES.
Damn it all. The only
poem i ever wrote
was called SHIRTS.
It was rejected by
Tailor and Cutter magazine
because although it was
called shirts it had
nothing to do with
shirts.
It was really
in an
oblique sort of way
a poem about Autumn

and dead leaves
piling up and
driving all
the road sweepers
to suicide. the
cruel irony of it was
that the leaves disappeared
anyway
even though
the sweepers were all
dead.
The point is
that everyone can be sure
that if I did
write a poem called
KNUCKLEBONES
it would be about
something else
entirely.
Perhaps I should
retitle this poem
KNUCKLEBONES.

A serious case of bardic fission

The identikit laureate
slips into his sweatshirt and trainers
6 a.m. sharp
hits the tarmac 5 m.p.h. jogging.
Much love in his heart
and a stiffy down below
of such noble resolution
could donate a considerable boost
to the power grid.
Why, he asks God, are we bombing
our global village?
That question, says God, shows
little understanding of village life.
Our sweaty identikit laureate
has a poem coming on in his head
provisionally entitled:
COOL SHIT ZIPS THRU THE FAN
LIKE PELLETS FROM A SYNCHRONISED
MACHINE GUN.
Poem features Satchmo, Fats, Bird
Miles, Dizzy and the goaties
all spruced up
in Hawaiian shirts, patent leathers
porkpie hats.
They dump orthodoxy in the duckpond.

Then they're up and away to send the
gates of heaven into meltdown.
           The sky, it so happens
is exactly the blue
that's an awful lot less that all ye
need to know about uranium rods
glowing in clear water.
           To the west a few patterns, vaguely
                                        grey
resembling men's white underpants
uncared for, occasionally left to soak
in scummy bathtubs
full of small hurt looks.

It so happens nothing much

true, they can still hit the charts
pack a stadium. but who would want
those old rockers' livers?
'slike asking who's lusting after
          my virgin octogenarian arse.
Can't speak for my contemporaries
                          they all
                          dead

or missing
presumed vaporised.
                          nothing much
is what it all comes down to
                          if
you stick around long enough –
                          certain

eventualities
will accrue   and
whether you're fatter or thinner
you'll know what it's like to be
                          invisible
          before you have
                    actually disappeared.

Women

women are a wild aroma thing
they befuddle and disaster a
man so he cant tell rite from
rong. i dont want to talk a-
bout the daughters of them old
chisellers the gods of the problems of how Adam swapped a good
ribsteak for a dish of acid
sprinkled with sweet bumfluff.
other writers write about this
much better than me an as a
result without any justification
tho the sky will fall on my
head for saying this. some of
my attributes have no affinities
with my other attributes and i
can't hold up the sky any longer
tho it's really under my feet.
that bitch Helen is a stupid
little bitch. i'd like to dunk
her in the tadpoles cos she
drinks ten flagons of Natch every day and is part of the local
demonology. she's shacked up
with old Cyclops a nasty old sod

who is one day a mad sheepdog
another day stinking swineherd.
there's no justice in the world.
the kids've cornered the soffdope
market and bought up all the condoms. car alarms are screaming all
night and there's nowhere else to
go. ow. i need a bad woman so bad!

Short story

Paul is in love with Debbie.
Debbie cross the ocean dies in a plane crash.
The news hits Paul off the fairway
he's dumped among the thorny brambles
where a loathsome Jungian shrink
happens to be picking blackberries
with uncanny synchronicity.
Ah says the shrink you're the split infinitudes
of a man in search of a soul.
Bunkum says Paul I'm a metaphor.
The ego and the shadow says the shrink
I shall re-write your prologue and epilogue.
Paul calms down perks up chills out
and has a dream which he forgets
and wakes up fully flared and resplendent of crotch.
Paul's sober reassessment of Debbie:
she was only a wax doll with designer eyelashes
who dabbled in hyperventilation
and called it new-age rebirthing.
She scrambled my eggs in lard silly bitch.
Suddenly without warning
Debbie returns from the dead in a terrible rage.
Damnation she yells
I missed that motherfucking plane.
It coulda been a peak experience.

Don't patronise me Paul you bastard she says
stop slobbering do something.
Get me a good hypnotist
I want to be deeply regressed.
Maybe I was on that plane after all
and what I am now is a reincarnation.
Paul paces the room focusing intently
and practicing vicious headbutts
on the palm of his hand.

Thin slices

My friend the artist
Is mixing paint
In a whirlpool
It's one of those days

He's harangued
By symmetry and cliches
Pious as terrorists

I used to loaf around
Beauty spots
Historical places
Then I got bored

They all looked the same
I slept in the car parks

Eventually
I never went anywhere
Stayed at home scribbling
Vicious little verses

And lo and behold

A luminous halo hovered

Over the dung-heap

He glares at the blank
Canvas
Blames it for everything
Attacks it with a steak knife

Caution down the sluice
Art at the cutting edge

My greatest pocm is a
Blood-smeared toilet tissue

I was shaving in a hurry
Got careless

Or lucky

Why agonise?

High on rust

Hilarious the course of eyeballs.
Crazy the forking of each other's poems.
You were in one of your lime-green
Merciful gossip periods.
                              I was in
My dark ruined interior ochre, the one
That invalided me out of the rat race.
You bequeathed me the pickle jar.
Then after we'd eaten our fingers
As many times as they chose to abate themselves
We contracted a severe dose of the monarchies.
Like the monarchies our plans went ping.
Suddenly rust became the currently beautiful thing.
Oh the vehemence and bizarre eloquence
Of rust's opposition to a long and healthy future.
We rolled on the floor and wept
For the haunted proprietors of rust-prone estate.
Drunk with our spoils we staggered out
Into the night sky, the bright beads and all
That has disappeared there.
                              Being ourselves
Also tarred with the invisible, we claimed
The right to be blasphemous and gave
The sign of the finger to the whole splurge.
Sign of the finger, even to the holy star.

Pointless rigmarole

Ladies and gentlemen
My apologies for being so long-winded
And still not getting to the point
That is, if there is a point
And if, indeed, it's a point worth making.
It's well known that by travelling west
One can arrive in the east.
But my antics are inexcusable:
I wander north, south, east, and west
And never arrive anywhere.
It's time to come clean.
The point I wish to make
Is that there's no point in anything
The whole cradle-to-grave rigmarole
Is absolutely pointless.
Most of us chatter like monkeys.
I – I have to confess –
Chatter enough for ten dozen –
On and on I go
Compulsively mouthing superfluous words
As if trying to make up for
A world shortage of the damn things –
Much like the people who breed like rabbits
While millions of kids are starving.
To believe that I'll ever stop talking

Is like expecting us all to stop fucking.
One day, of course,
Death or something worse will stop my gob
 – And ultimately everything will stop.
I may as well have said that in the first place.